DREAMS AND VISIONS

Understanding the Language of the Spirit

Bob Griffin

A Dream or a Vision is God's Invitation to a Relationship!

A Note of Thanks....

All my love, all my heart, all my soul, and all my thanks to the Creator of the Universe for His invitation to know Him in an intimate way. Thank You Jesus!

I would like to thank my lovely wife, Jayne, a **true** Proverbs 31 woman, and my four children, Jasmine, Jordan, Joel and Rachael for their love and support and prayers!

Love, Daddy

To the wonderful staff at LCMI who continually bless us with their prayers of support and have chosen to go the distance with God!

DREAMS AND VISIONS

Copyright © 2002 Life Changes Ministries International
ISBN 0-9728661-9-1

First Printing 2003

This book and other resources are available online at
WWW.BOBGRIFFINWORLD.COM....keyword Resources.
2nd Generation Media Group
P.O. Box 153 * New Boston, MI 48164
For speaking invitations, please call LCMI offices at
(734) 782-5128 or fax (734) 782-5194.

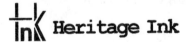 **Heritage Ink**

2933 Madison Street, Marianna, Florida 32446

Printed in the United States of America

Contents

Preface

Introduction:..11

Chapter 1:
God's DNA..15

Chapter 2:
Your Dream Seed..29

Chapter 3:
Symbols...41

Chapter 4:
Interpretation of Symbols..65

Dreams and Visions

Introduction

I was first introduced to dreams at twelve years of age, and at the time of this writing over thirty years have passed. I can still recall a dream I had thirty-one years ago. It is still a picture embedded in my spirit that has at times redirected me back to the will of God for my life, and because of its nature, it has helped me to stay *God focused*. Ironically, in today's world there are seasons when I have difficulty remembering details of a dream. However, there are other times that within moments of awakening, I recognize the dreams that are *God given*. These stand out with clarity, sometimes with color and smells. Even feelings of compassion well up at the recalling of some of these dream seeds. These are answers to prayers that have been given in the season of the night as prophetic speech.

Dreams and Visions

Mysteries are swirling within our being. Even our hearts are veiled from the mysteries of God, and while this book is the beginning of only one step into the discovery of purpose for our lives, my prayer is that you will begin to tap into the spirit realm of the Creator of the Universe and discover mysteries about yourself.

I believe that in this day, many books could be written on the subject of *Dreams and Visions*. Yet, as frequent as God is speaking through dreams today, our understanding seems to be veiled. So we have endeavored to begin to release *a word in due season*, that we all may begin to enter in beyond the veil of limitations. I believe that a dream or a vision is an invitation to a relationship.

As a prophetic dreamer of dreams, I pray this book will help you capture a glimpse into the heart of God, while still enjoying the journey home. My home is in another world, one not formed by human hands. It's my desire to know the One who is, and was, and is to come. And while not all dreams are prophetic or spiritual in nature, I do believe we can all learn from our dreams, if we just take the time to ask.

> *So I say to you, ask, and it will be given to you; seek, and you will find; knock, and it will be opened to you.*
>
> *Luke 11:9*

Dreams and Visions

Chapter One

God's DNA

Be glad then, you children of Zion, and rejoice in the Lord your God; for He has given you the former rain faithfully, and He will cause the rain to come down for you—the former rain, and the latter rain in the first month.

The threshing floors shall be full of wheat, and the vats shall overflow with new wine and oil.

So I will restore to you the years that the swarming locust has eaten, the crawling locust, the consuming locust, and the chewing locust, My great army which I sent among you.

You shall eat in plenty and be satisfied, and praise the name of the Lord your God, who has dealt wondrously with you; and My people shall never be put to shame.

Then you shall know that I am in the midst of Israel; I am the Lord your God and there is no other. My people shall never be put to shame.

Dreams and Visions

And it shall come to pass afterward that I will pour out My Spirit on all flesh; your sons and your daughters shall prophesy, your old men shall dream dreams, your young men shall see visions.

And also on My menservants and on My maid-servants I will pour out My Spirit in those days.

And I will show wonders in the heavens and in the earth: Blood and fire and pillars of smoke.

The sun shall be turned into darkness, and the moon into blood, before the coming of the great and awesome day of the Lord.

And it shall come to pass that whoever calls on the name of the Lord shall be saved. For in Mount Zion and in Jerusalem there shall be deliverance, as the Lord has said, among the remnants whom the Lord calls.

Joel 2:23-32

We see a picture of restoration wherein Joel says that food is cut off.

Has not food been cut off before our eyes, gladness and joy from the house of our God?

Joel 1:16

The seeds shrivel under their clods (no water); the storehouses are desolate (no order); the barns are torn down (no oversight) for the grain is dried up (food and future food).

Joel 1:17

16

*How the animals groan! (hunger has seized them)
the herds of cattle are restless (fear and anxiety)
because they have no pasture (good shepherds
lead to new fields and food) even the flocks of
sheep suffer punishment (are made desolate under harsh rule).*

Joel 1:18

*O Lord, to you I cry out; for fire has devoured
the open pastures (pastures of the wilderness)
and a flame has burned all the trees of the field.*

Joel 1:19

*Call upon Me in the day of trouble; I will deliver
you and you shall glorify Me.*

Psalm 50:15

Jeremiah 9:7-26 speaks to us of the heart.

*Therefore thus says the Lord of hosts, "Behold I
will refine them and try them; for how shall I deal
with the daughter of My people?*

*Their tongue is an arrow shot out; it speaks de-
ceit; one speaks peaceably to his neighbor with
his mouth, but in his heart he lies in wait.*

*"Shall I not punish them for these things?" says
the Lord. "Shall I not avenge Myself on such a
nation as this?"*

*I will take up a weeping and wailing for the moun-
tains, and for the dwelling places of the wilderness a lamentation, because they are burned up,
so that no one can pass through; nor can men
hear the voice of the cattle. Both the birds of the
heavens and the beasts have fled; they are gone.*

17

Dreams and Visions

"I will make Jerusalem a heap of ruins, a den of jackals. I will make the cities of Judah desolate, without an inhabitant."

Who is the wise man who may understand this? And who is he to whom the mouth of the Lord has spoken, that he may declare it? Why does the land perish and burn up like a wilderness, so that no one can pass through?

And the Lord said, "Because they have forsaken My law which I set before them, and have not obeyed My voice, nor walked according to it,

"but they have walked according to the dictates of their own hearts and after the Baals, which their fathers taught them,"

therefore thus says the Lord of hosts, the God of Israel, "Behold I will feed them, this people, with wormwood and give them water of gall to drink.

"I will scatter them also among the Gentiles, whom neither they nor their fathers have known. And I will send a sword after them until I have consumed them."

Thus says the Lord of hosts, "Consider and call for the mourning women, that they may come; and send for skillful wailing women, that they may come!

Let them make haste, and take up a wailing for us, that our eyes may run with tears, and our eyelids gush with water.

For a voice of wailing is heard from Zion, 'How we are plundered! We are greatly ashamed, because we have forsaken the land, because we have been cast out of our dwellings.'"

Yet hear the word of the Lord, O women, and let your ear receive the word of His mouth; teach your daughters wailing, and everyone her neighbor a lamentation.

For death has come through our windows; has entered our palaces, to kill off the children no longer to be outside! And the young men no longer on the streets!

Speak, "Thus says the Lord: 'Even the carcasses of men shall fall as refuge on the open field, like cuttings after the harvester, and no one shall gather them.'"

Thus says the Lord, "Let not the wise man glory in his wisdom, let not the mighty man glory in his might, nor let the rich man glory in his riches;

But let him who glories glory in this, that he understands and knows Me, that I am the Lord exercising lovingkindness, judgment, and righteousness in the earth; for in these I delight," declares the Lord.

"Behold, the days are coming," says the Lord, "that I will punish all who are circumcised with the uncircumcised —

"Egypt, Judah, Edom, the people of Ammon, Moab, and all who are in the farthest corners, who dwell in the wilderness. For all these nations are uncircumcised, and all the house of Israel are uncircumcised in the heart."

Jeremiah 9:7-26

He portrays a people that have refused to surrender to the will of God. Jeremiah was divinely called and inspired as a youth, even a young man. He was a <u>broken-hearted</u> prophet with a <u>heartbreaking</u> message. For over forty years, Jeremiah labored proclaiming a message of tearing down to build. God called him as a youth, and the Word of the Lord <u>came to him</u> saying:

Dreams and Visions

"Before I formed you in the womb, I knew you; before you were born, I sanctified you! (set you apart) I ordained (appointed) you a prophet to the nations."

Then said I: "Ah, Lord God! Behold I cannot speak, for I am a youth."

But the Lord said to me: 'Do not say, 'I am a youth,' for you shall go to all to whom I send you, and whatever I command you, you shall speak.

"Do not be afraid of their faces, for I am with you to deliver you," says the Lord.

Jeremiah 1:5-8

God sends us into places we fear to go and then proclaims *I am with you to deliver you!* That deliverance is from fear, and as a messenger. God's hidden speech can be quiet, stern, or amusing, as we will learn. God called Jeremiah from the heart, from the depths of his hidden resources. God's **DNA** is in each one of us.

You are sons of the prophets, and of the covenant which God made with our fathers, saying to Abraham, 'And in your seed all the families of the earth shall be blessed.'

Acts 3:25

Now to Abraham and his Seed were the promises made...

Galatians 3:16

He does not say, *and to seeds*, as of many, but as of one, *and to your seed, who is Christ*.

> *And says "As he spoke to our fathers, to Abraham and to his seed forever."*
>
> *Luke 1:55*

The divine nature of the Almighty is inside of you, waiting for destiny, faith, hope, love, desperation, persecution, tribulation, sorrow, hopelessness and despair to collide into the one split second of energy that forces the seed of faith, that incorruptible seed of God's nature to spring forth into a kingdom warrior that thirsts for the outpouring of God's Word. That outpouring is **His Spirit** that waters, **His Presence** that nurtures, **His Manifold Wisdom** that teaches, **His Love** that leads us out of fear, and out of sin-thinking.

> *Having been born again, not of corruptible seed but incorruptible, through the word of God which lives and abides forever.*
>
> *1 Peter 1:23*

21

Dreams and Visions

Both death and life are in the seed. When God's <u>mercy</u> called Jeremiah to not be afraid of their faces, I believe He was saying *When you see the priests who are ever changing in their demeanor, who, one moment are like a bear who tears, or a lion who roars, or a serpent who bites, or a jackal who cackles...**Go beyond their faces** and cut to the heart from where all hidden and harsh agendas flow. Where a brokenness can reach in and declare 'thus says the Lord.'* Tear down, build, root out and plant. For God says *I will deliver you. I am with you to deliver you!*

> *Then the Lord put forth His Hand and touched my mouth, and the Lord said to me: "Behold, I have put My words in your mouth.*
>
> *See, I have this day set you over the nations and over the kingdoms, to root out and to pull down, to destroy and to throw down, to build and to plant."*
>
> Jeremiah 1:9-10

> *But may the God of all grace, who called us to His eternal glory by Christ Jesus, after you have suffered a while, perfect, establish, strengthen, and settle you.*
>
> 1 Peter 5:10

So in essence, you need to allow God to **root out,** so He can **perfect, pull down, establish, destroy, strengthen,** and **throw down**, so He can **settle you.** Then you will find yourself **built** and **planted** by His hand. This is really and truly a blessing to be torn down and then rebuilt. The renewal process must be embraced to be effectual in His Kingdom.

> "I will deliver you from all your uncleanness. I will call for the grain and multiply it, and bring no famine upon you.
>
> "And I will multiply the fruit of your trees and the increase of your fields, so that you need never again bear the reproach of famine among the nations.
>
> "Then you will remember your evil ways and your deeds that were not good; and you will loathe yourselves in your own sight, for your iniquities and your abominations.
>
> "Not for your sake do I do this," says the Lord God, "let it be known to you. Be ashamed and confounded for your own ways, O house of Israel!"
>
> 'Thus says the Lord God: "On the day that I cleanse you from all your iniquities, I will also enable you to dwell in the cities, and the ruins shall be rebuilt.
>
> "The desolate land shall be tilled instead of lying desolate in the sight of all who pass by.
>
> "So they will say, 'This land that was desolate has become like the garden of Eden; and the wasted, desolate, and ruined cities are now fortified and inhabited.' "

> *Then the nations which are left all around you shall know that I, the Lord, have rebuilt the ruined places and planted what was desolate. I, the Lord, have spoken it, and I will do it."*
>
> *'Thus says the Lord God: "I will also let the house of Israel inquire of Me to do this for them: I will increase their men like a flock.*
>
> *"Like a flock offered as holy sacrifices, like the flock of Jerusalem on its feast days, so shall the ruined cities be filled with flocks of men. Then they shall know that I am the Lord."*
>
> Ezekiel 36:29-38

Though the process is painful, the latter end is God's glory to establish true headship in our lives.

> *"I will establish one shepherd over them, and he shall feed them—My servant David. He shall feed them and be their shepherd.*
>
> *"And I, the Lord, will be their God, and My servant David a prince among them; I, the Lord, have spoken."*
>
> *"I will make a covenant of peace with them, and cause wild beasts to cease from the land; and they will dwell safely in the wilderness and sleep in the woods.*
>
> *"I will make them and the places all around My hill a blessing; and I will cause showers to come down in their season; there shall be showers of blessing.*
>
> *"Then the trees of the field shall yield their fruit, and the earth shall yield her increase. They shall be safe in their land; and they shall know that I*

am the Lord, when I have broken the bands of their yoke and delivered them from the hand of those who enslaved them.

"And they shall no longer be a prey for the nations, nor shall beasts of the land devour them; but they shall dwell safely, and no one shall make them afraid.

"I will raise up for them a garden of renown, and they shall no longer be consumed with hunger in the land, nor bear the shame of the Gentiles anymore.

"Thus they shall know that I, the Lord their God, am with them, and they, the house of Israel are My people," says the Lord God.'" "You are My flock, the flock of My pasture; you are men, and I am your God," says the Lord God.

Ezekiel 34:23-31

Then we begin to see God's ways—hear God's voice—see God's vision!

Moreover, the word of the Lord came to me, saying, "Jeremiah, what do you see?" And I said, "I see a branch of an almond tree."

Then the Lord said to me, "You have seen well, for I am ready to perform My word."

And the word of the Lord came to me the second time, saying "What do you see?" And I said, "I see a boiling pot, and it's facing away from the north."

Jeremiah 1:11

The symbol of a branch of an almond tree and the boiling pot, cries out for interpretation. Even the direction it pours from and to, all express ideas from God. In Israel, the almond tree is an early blossoming fruit tree that blossoms before other trees, even awakened from dormancy. It speaks to us of Aaron's rod, which symbolizes a rod of authority in the hands of a prophet, thus, a tree that bears fruit out of season. We will cover other symbols throughout the teachings.

He removes our voice and our ideas in exchange for His thoughts—this is where we must allow God to exchange our image for His. In this opening of a book of destiny, through Jeremiah, God speaks louder to the prophetic generation of today than any generation before. God chooses a child to speak and demonstrate to a generation of stiff-necked people of Judah. He becomes despised and persecuted by his own people, all the while bathing his prophecies of tearing down with tears of compassion. Through his preaching, teaching, and signs and wonders, he faithfully declares God's heart by calling the people to surrender their wills to God's will or receive the calamity and doom of the prophetic word.

Dreams and Visions

Chapter Two

Your Dream Seed

Yirmeyahu, or *Jeremiah,* literally means *Yahweh throws,* perhaps in the sense of laying a foundation. It may effectively mean *Yahweh es-tablishes, appoints, or sends.* When God speaks in a vision or a dream, a picture is worth a thousand years. More than a thousand words could be spoken of any image. Images are pictures captured for a moment and retained for a lifetime of learning and inquiring. When Joel prophesied that the food is cut off (speaks of spiritual food before our eyes, such as dreams and visions), all joy and gladness from the house of God was cut off. It speaks of no relationship. The seed shriveling under the clods is a prophetic image of God's promise lying dormant under a dry heart with no faith. In reality, He desires you to be planted as a noble vine, a seed of highest quality [Jeremiah 2:21-22]. He asks, *How then have you turned before Me into the degenerate plant of an alien vine? God's desire is to plant you in His house; to water you by His Spirit.*

Moses and the children of Israel sang this song to the Lord, and spoke saying,

> *'You will bring them in and plant them in the mountain of your inheritance. In the place, O Lord, which you have made for your own dwelling, the sanctuary, O Lord, which your hands have established.*
>
> *Exodus 15:17*

It is God's hand, His arm and the light of His countenance that plants us.

> *For they did not gain possession of the land by their own sword, nor did their own arm save them; but it was Your right hand, Your arm, and the light of Your countenance, because You favored them.*
>
> *Psalm 44:3*

We are planted and watered as <u>we worship God</u>. Take away worship and you will be burnt out, broken apart, dried up, shriveled up and desolate. A seed has more than <u>one</u> need. It must have light, water and heat. To have one without the other there can be no life. Wherever there is a seed there is a need. Wherever there is a need there is a seed! This is a word of wisdom! Bury it in your heart. You will need this wisdom forever!

When God waters you, it is because you water Him. When you bathe Him in worship, He will water the dream seeds within you!

The Lord will command His lovingkindness in the daytime, and in the night His song shall be with me—a prayer to the God of my life.

Psalm 42:8

Worship releases adoration and praise, and God releases relationship and revelation — *Love and Light.* Tears water our soul and touch His heart. He releases His Word which waters our seeds. We release love, and He releases His Spirit, which comforts and warms. Thus, LOVE [nurturing] and LIGHT [countenance] and WATER [Word] and COMPASSION [the comforter who warms], light, water and warmth are all found in a relationship.

Isaiah 41:17-20 is a prophetic picture of all seven churches planted together and being watered.

Dreams and Visions

The poor and needy seek water, but there is none, their tongues fail for thirst. I, the Lord, will hear them; I, the God of Israel, will not forsake them.

I will open rivers in desolate heights, and fountains in the midst of the valleys; I will make the wilderness a pool of water, and the dry land springs of water.

I will plant in the wilderness the cedar and the acacia tree, the myrtle and the oil tree; I will set in the desert the cypress tree and the pine and the box tree together,

That they may see and know, and consider and understand together, that the hand of the Lord has done this, and the Holy One of Israel has created it.

Isaiah 41:17-20

We must cry out for restoration.

Restore us, O God of Hosts; cause Your face to shine (light), and we shall be saved.

You have brought a vine out of Egypt; You have cast out the nations, and planted it.

You prepared room for it and caused it to take deep root, and it filled the land.

The hills were covered with its shadow, and the mighty cedars with its boughs.

She sent out her boughs to the sea, and her branches to the River.

Why have you broken down her hedges, so that all who pass by the way pluck her fruit?

The boar out of the woods uproots it and the wild beast of the field devours it.

Return, we beseech You, O God of hosts; Look down from heaven and see, and visit the vine

And the vineyard which Your right hand has planted, and the branch that You made strong for Yourself.

It is burned with fire, it is cut down; they perish at the rebuke of Your countenance.

Let Your hand be upon the man of Your right hand, upon the son of man whom You made strong for Yourself.

Then we will not turn back from You; Revive us [water us] and we will call upon Your name.

Restore us, O Lord God of hosts; cause Your face to shine [light], and we shall be saved [warmed]."

Psalm 80:7-19

Again, water, light and warmth! This prophetic prayer for Israel's restoration became a song, a psalm and a testimony. Stir up your strength and come and save us. Water our hearts that we may dream the dreams of kings and prophets! Child-like faith ignites our hearts to sing and then be watered. Jesus is the only minister I know who thanked His Father for hiding His message from the audience at large, when He thanked His Father for hiding it from the wise and prudent, and revealing it to babies.

At that time Jesus answered and said, "I thank You, Father, You have hidden these things from the wise and prudent and have revealed them to babes.

"Even so, Father, for so it seemed good in Your sight.

"All things have been delivered to Me by My Father, and no one knows the Son except the Father. Nor does anyone know the Father except the Son, and the one to whom the Son wills to reveal Him.

"Come to Me, all you who labor and are heavy-laden, and I will give you rest.

"Take My yoke upon you and learn from Me, for I am gentle and lowly in heart, and you will find rest for your souls.

"For My yoke is easy and My burden is light."

Matthew 11:25-30

Hearing also comes from God. Let us hear what the Spirit has to say. Jesus' burden is light, and light also speaks of revelation. It is interesting that restoration involves both seeing and hearing.

Acts 3:19-21 says that repentance will bring forth times of refreshing from the presence of the Lord. also, that He may send Jesus Christ who was preached to you before, whom heaven must receive UNTIL THE TIMES OF RESTORATION of all things, which GOD HAS SPOKEN by the mouth of all HIS HOLY PROPHETS since the world began.

When Jesus told the disciples to tarry or wait for *the promise of the Father which you have heard from Me*, it was not heard about, but rather, <u>demonstrated</u>.

> *And He said to them, "It is not for you to know times or season which the Father has put in His own authority.*
>
> *"But you shall receive power when the Holy Spirit has come upon you; and you shall be witnesses to Me in Jerusalem, and in all Judea and Samaria, and to the ends of the earth."*
>
> *Acts 1:7-8*

Jesus said, *It is not for you to know times or seasons* which the Father has put in His authority, but you shall receive power *when the Holy Spirit has come upon you,* (for what?) to be witnesses *AND* to know times and seasons. My prayer is for prophetic impartation to help raise up a prophetic generation of dreamers who both hear and see.

> *And suddenly there came a sound from heaven, as of a rushing mighty wind, and it filled the whole house where they were sitting.*
>
> *Then there appeared to them divided tongues, as of fire, and one sat upon each of them.*

35

> *And they were all filled with the Holy Spirit and
> began to speak with other tongues, as the Spirit
> gave them utterance."*
>
> *Acts 2:2-4*

There came a <u>sound</u> from heaven that filled the place where they were sitting. Then there <u>appeared</u> to them divided tongues, as of fire—they heard, they saw, and they were filled. Peter declared in Acts 1:14-18, that the evidence of that true experience is that we will <u>hear, see, be filled, prophesy, see visions, dream dreams, and be shown wonders in heaven above and signs in the earth beneath.</u>

> *These all continued with one accord in prayer and
> supplication, with the women and Mary the mother
> of Jesus, and with His brothers.*
>
> *And in those days Peter stood up in the midst of
> the disciples [altogether the number of names
> was about a hundred and twenty] and said,*
>
> *"Men and brethren, this Scripture had to be ful-
> filled, which the Holy Spirit spoke before by the
> mouth of David concerning Judas, who became a
> guide to those who arrested Jesus;*
>
> *"for he was numbered with us and obtained a
> part in this ministry."*
>
> *[Now this man purchased a field with the wages
> of iniquity; and falling headlong, he burst open in
> the middle and all his entrails gushed out]."*
>
> *Acts 1:14-18*

When God plants you on the mountain of His inheritance, He is saying to all of heaven and all of earth: ***Touch not my anointed and do My prophets no harm...***

When they went from one nation to another, from one kingdom to another people,

He permitted no one to do them wrong; Yes, He rebuked kings for their sakes,

Saying, "Do not touch My anointed ones, and do My prophets no harm."

Psalm 105:13-15

"Yet I have set My King on My holy hill of Zion."

"I will declare the decree: The Lord has said to Me, 'You are My Son, today I have begotten You.

Ask of Me, and I will give <u>you</u> the nations as an <u>inheritance, and the ends of the earth for your possession</u>.

You shall break them with a rod of iron; you shall dash them to pieces like a potter's vessel.'"

"Now therefore, be wise, O Kings; Be instructed, you judges of the earth. Serve the Lord with fear, and rejoice with trembling.

<u>Kiss the Son</u>, lest He be angry, and you perish in the way, when His wrath is kindled but a little. Blessed are all those who put their trust in Him."

Psalm 2:6-12

Zion is the place of the outpouring! It is the mountain of God's love, the building of His tabernacle, the planting of His hand, the watering of His Spirit. It is God's desire to grant you authority to rule and reign as sons on the earth, as kings and judges. Yet all of this is progressive as we begin to yield to God and allow Him to restore us both to Him and to one another.

> *"And he who overcomes, and keeps My works until the end, to him I will give power over the nations—*
>
> *'He shall rule them with a rod of iron; they shall be dashed to pieces like the potter's vessels' — as I also have received from My Father;*
>
> *"and I will give him the morning star.*
>
> *"He who has an ear, let him hear what the Spirit says to the churches."'*
>
> *Revelation 2:26-29*

Our rod of iron is truth. This is a prophetic picture and call from <u>God</u> to <u>us,</u> to truly overcome fear, sickness, sin, iniquities, and come into right relationship with Him as sons and daughters, that we might truly *come* over into blessings, authority, power, and into the full measure. A rod speaks of authority and truth, for breaking open *jars of clay*, or our flesh. A prophetic word, vision or dream from God, carries an anointing to break open, to pull down, to root out, to destroy, to throw down, to build (or rebuild) and to plant. Iron speaks of military power or authority. In other words, a kingdom anointing for restoration, correction and edification is found in God's language. Whatever comes from God returns to God, and is not diminished in authority or power. His true desire is to restore us to Him. This is ultimately every true prophet's dream; to see humanity reconciled with God through Christ.

I believe this word can ignite your soul, and water your dream seed, break up the fallow ground, and generate faith to grow when heard through ears to hear. When God calls you a son...your sonship is consecrated. You are now sanctified to rule, and anointed to speak. You will rule, you will reign, you will succeed as a seed in His kingdom. You are now a divine vine; a rod of iron in the hand of God.

A vision can show you who you are, what you'll be, how to rule, what to say, and in the night God seals our instructions...as He waters us with the dew.

> Then He opens the ears of men, and seals
> their instruction.
>
> Job 33:16

Jeremiah both heard and saw because his heart did not condemn him. We must endeavor to see

39

God's restoration take place in us before we move to the beginning of this *Word in due season.* Worship waters the dream seeds that are resident within us, and yet God can choose to reveal Himself sovereignly as He did to Joseph, to Jacob, to Peter or Saul.

Chapter Three

Symbols

Dreams and Visions are the hidden language of the Spirit that communicate His mind and will to His people. Because we often do not know our own hearts, He will use hidden speech, enigmas, proverbs, dark sayings, parables, dreams or visions to reveal secrets or hidden truths. Deep calls out to deep. If we pay careful attention to details, scenes, and symbols, we may be able to properly interpret the meaning of the dream or its message for a proper application. In the many years of teaching on this subject, I feel I have only just begun to scratch the surface of understanding and to pray that this journey will continue as God leads me to deeper understanding. I do attempt, whenever possible, to line both the dream and its interpretation up with Scripture. In so doing, my spirit-man, or kingdom-figure, begins to think as He thinks. This is not always possible considering the vast number of symbols or types that are now given to us in the vernacular of today's language. However, the principles are present a vast majority of the time, and for me, I prefer to see line upon line and precept upon precept.

Symbols and their meanings can change definitions from one season to another. This growth is progressive, and because He is the voice of *many waters*, His images continue to give life and teach even as Scripture is seen in new light as we grow into the full stature of Christ, to a perfect man, to the measure of the stature of fullness of Christ. HIS WORD IS THE TRUE PLUMBLINE!

Symbols alone, are not enough to interpret a dream. We must know something about the subject of the dream or be familiar with the person's background. We must never attempt to interpret a dream for ourselves or another without first asking the Holy Spirit for His truth. While some symbols may become universally understood, their application may vary from person to person or even season to season.

In order to navigate correctly, we must take the time to ponder, to listen, and record the dream for future insight. A dream journal is very helpful if we include date/time, and even where we were in that season. It allows us to return and give more insight to its meaning.

In the Hebrew dialect, the word *Chalam* means to recover; to restore to health.

> CHALAM, KHAW-LAM; *Strongs* #2492—recover. *To recover—lit. means to get back (something lost or stolen, etc.) to regain (health) to make up for (to recover losses) to save (oneself) from a fall.*
>
> Recovery = a return to health; a regaining of something lost (as in relationship).
>
> Recovery room = a hospital room where post-operative patients are kept for close observation and care.
>
> *Websters New World Dictionary of the American Language, Modern Desk Edition* (1976, 1979). Simon E. Shuster.

Our imagination serves as a receiver to unfold our future, and as we weigh this with Scripture and a seasoned mentor, we are actually in a position to grow and heal from hidden wounds or hurts that manifest indirectly and are otherwise hidden from us. God cares enough to recover us and save us when we are falling.

The word SYMBOL comes from two Greek words which mean *to throw together*. In dreams, we are free to experience an incredible awareness of His beauty and glory. In our imagination, we possess the ability to contemplate or incubate, to think heavily upon the object of our affection. By throwing together many symbols, our active imagination is able to think, reason and deduce. However, when God's creativity begins to throw together metaphors, hidden speech, symbols and dark sayings, we must reason that someone beyond us is speaking.

These symbols are now words. Much like a Word of Knowledge, a vision or symbol is able to speak of something hidden. Feelings can also represent symbols. A pain in the knee is symbolic of an injury. Or a sound such as a whistle or buzz can speak to us of an ear problem. Thus, His speech includes all areas of our senses and shouldn't be limited to just our seeing but also smell, touch, sight, sound, taste and even feeling. The images we experience represent a vast spiritual harvest by which we are able to glean spiritual truth.

Symbols or words can represent our past, present, or future state of mind, as well as reveal feelings relating to moods. Generally speaking, your dreams are telling you something about yourself as they communicate something to your body, soul, and spirit. All symbols are important and should be recorded. Symbols are also universal, as in a dove, a symbol of peace or hope—with an olive branch, which speaks of peace, or covenant in Israel—which is also scriptural.

> *Then the dove came to him in the evening, and behold, a freshly plucked olive leaf was in her mouth; and Noah knew that the waters had abated from the earth.*
>
> *Genesis 8:11*

Seasons of your life are also symbolic. Anger, hurts, bitterness and unforgiveness can actually cut you off from receiving God's Word for your life. And yet God may choose to restore you to health...to recover your covenant relationship.

Psalm 73:20-24 is a spiritual picture of a heart condition.

> *As a dream when one awakes, So, Lord, when You awake, You shall despise their image.*
>
> *Thus my heart was grieved, and I was vexed in my mind.*
>
> *I was so foolish and ignorant; I was like a beast before You.*
>
> *Nevertheless I am continually with You; You hold me by my right hand.*
>
> *You will guide me with Your counsel, and afterward receive me to glory.*
>
> *Psalm 73:20-24*

Anger and bitterness can actually cut us off from perceiving God, when our hearts condemn us or our conscience is hardened. We are sometimes aware and simply choose to ignore God, choosing our *own* feelings instead. The word conscience means, *with knowledge*.

I knew an individual who felt utterly rejected by everyone, and because of this pain, withdrew into a dark pit within the heart. Feeling separated from God, and withdrawing further from all relationships, he began to forget who he was in Christ. Transgression and sin followed. Rebellion began to lead him into a path of destruction. One night he dreamed a dream for which I was called upon to interpret. The dream scene came quickly. In the first scene, he was driving like a mad man over hills and around dangerous curves until suddenly his vehicle left the ground and was airborne in a free fall (speaks of being out of control). There were various pot holes and deep pits in the road. When the vehicle finally landed, he had passed over many pits. However, at the end of the road was a band playing a weird demonic song. The band was all dressed in black and orange and it was very dark and lonely there. I would say this dream was very easy to interpret. However, we must also take the time to know the individual and look at the circumstances. I gave you the circumstances for the dream, how would you interpret the symbols?

God said He would counsel us and guide us, and afterward receive us into glory. This was actually both a <u>warning</u> and a <u>deliverance</u>. Our bitterness or anger can actually cut off our senses. Thus the phrases: *I was blinded by anger. I was blind with rage.* A mind-blinding spirit could *drive us* down a path of rebellion (witchcraft) where there are many pitfalls. (Black and orange speaks of witches, Halloween, etc.). Satan was actually playing the strings of this man's heart, drawing him into despair because of sin, unconfessed anger, and unforgiveness.

I once spent time with a young woman who recalled a dream at lunch one day. She said in the dream that she visited a kind, white-haired doctor who was smiling over the end of his clipboard. Suddenly his demeanor changed as he eyed her lying on the examining table. He appeared to be following a checklist replying *Good, very good, yes, good,* until suddenly he said *Hmmmm, hmmm.* Feeling on the spot, the girl asked *Is there a problem?* The doctor replied *Could be, could be.* She asked *What is it?* He replied *Your gallbladder may need attention.* Fearing an actual physical problem, she awakened realizing she had just dreamed a dream.

Upon awakening, she began to ask, seek and knock for several days, desiring to know the answer.

Suddenly she had a thought to look up in the *Webster's Dictionary* the definition of *gallbladder*. In it she found Daniel Webster had recorded in her edition as one possible definition...SPIRIT OF BITTERNESS OR BITTER FEELING. Shocked, she asked the Lord if this was a problem, He replied *It could be!* She then asked, *What is the root?* He replied that because she was now in her thirties, and very attractive, yet still single, she had inwardly become bitter toward someone. She then asked *Who?* He replied *Me.* She quickly repented and was <u>restored</u>.

I have found that God will speak to us in our own language. To a doctor, He may use a metaphor, a figure of speech in which one thing is spoken of as if it were another. (Example: The curtain of night = speaking of darkness being a temporary veil). To a plumber, He may use pipes and fittings; to a golfer, clubs and phrases; to an ex-junkie, drug paraphernalia. I have seen God use specific words found only in one version of a dictionary available only in that house at that time, as well as seeing Him speak out of one particular version of the Bible. Recently, I saw the Lord speak of rubies, which were only found in a particular version, which happened to be the version available at the time of the dream.

Symbols, types and shadows are all a hidden language designed to nurture us back to a face to face relationship with God. Intimacy is really <u>IN—TO—ME—SEE</u>, and that is what God is wanting from all of us. This language is developed by God over time, as we allow Him to speak secrets, hidden moments that will ultimately restore us both to Him, to ourselves (we are sometimes fragmented by pain) and to others. They speak warnings and restoration.

I personally went through a difficult period in my life and sought God's help in my heart. While praying for release into the harvest field, many, many years ago, I fell asleep in my easy chair praying in tongues. Suddenly, I dreamed a very brightly-clothed young man (angel) came up the stairs into my living room and crossed over to my right side and bent over me as he placed a stethoscope over my heart. I asked him, *What are you doing here?* He replied, *Just checking for murmurs.* Suddenly, I awakened knowing that murmuring and complaining had to cease. When I asked the Lord to explain, He told me that I had been offended by the church. Still not fully aware of the potential problem, I thought *Well, that's true enough.* Suddenly, He said *The Church is My Bride.* Reality set in, and I realized that I was actually complaining to Him about *His wife.* That was a wake-up call to see as He sees. Thus, He recovers and He restores to health = Chalam-dream.

God indeed counsels us and then afterward receives us into glory.

> *You will guide me with Your counsel, and afterward receive me to glory.*
>
> *Psalm 73:24*

Anger, bitterness, and complaining, are all sin nature and in need of restoration. This is when the Counselor can actually lead us back into fellowship and communion with the Father by redirecting our senses which can be cut off by vows, hurts or disappointments. Dreams can be very therapeutic and revealing as the Great Physician who cares, truly shepherds our souls.

Pride is often a root of bitterness or anger, and misunderstandings often cause us to question God. He doesn't need to answer us. However, He often will reveal His heart because of His deep love for us. In Job 33, Elihu contradicts Job, and in verses 13-18 rebukes him, saying:

> *Why do you contend with Him? For He does not give an accounting of any of His words.*
>
> *For God may speak in one way, or in another, yet man does not perceive it.*
>
> *In a dream, in a vision of the night, when deep sleeps falls upon men, while slumbering on their beds,*

*Then He opens the ears of men, and seals their
instruction.*

*In order to turn man from his deed, and conceal
pride from man,*

*He keeps back his soul from the pit, and his life
from perishing by the sword.*

Job 33:13-18

God will bring deliverance to you and suddenly
change seasons in your life with only one word, or
one dream. And while God desires to keep you
from the pit, He also allows others to toss you into
the pit. At these times, He allows them to serve His
purpose to advance you in His plan to the next stage
of life, or platform. This is a healthy experience and
causes growth to the kingdom-figure inside of you!

God's intervention is deep, and should be viewed
from more than one perspective. He will sometimes
allow others to rebuke and chasten you in order to
cause you to grow, but be cautious when you are the
instrument. Their growth may supersede yours, and
thus you will now become the target for the pit.

Prophets are formed in the pit, and many dreamers are destined for this type of training. Joseph
who is famous for his dreams, was despised for them
as well. Let's look at God's training and even the
instruments of His purpose. Remember God seals
instructions as He opens the ears of men.

Dreams and Visions

*Then He opens the ears of men, and seals
their instruction.*

Job 33:16

*"Behold, God works all these things, twice,
in fact, three times with a man,*

*To bring back his soul from the Pit, that he may
be enlightened with the light of life."*

Job 33:29-30

When Joseph's brothers heard Joseph's dreams, they began to despise Him. It didn't help that his own father was the instrument for setting Joseph up for the fall. When the fall is great, so is the destiny intended. When Joseph's brothers proclaimed *Here, look, this dreamer is coming,* they were actually using a little known phrase as a slur meaning... *Look, this 'so-called master/leader' is coming.* Yet God literally *sent a man before them—Joseph—who was sold as a slave.* Look at Psalm 105:17-22:

*He sent a man before them-Joseph-who was sold
as a slave.*

They hurt his feet with fetters, he was laid in irons,

*Until the time that his word came to pass, the
word of the Lord tested him.*

*The king sent and released him, the ruler of the
people let him go free.*

*He made him lord of his house, and ruler of all
his possessions,*

*To bind his princes at his pleasure, and teach his
elders wisdom.*

Psalm 105:17-22

Remember, if you are the instrument that throws one in a pit, one day their growth may supersede yours and thus you will now become the target to be bound or placed in the pit.

God gives words and symbols in dreams to help us see the past, the present or the future, yet I believe it is almost always for us to learn something hidden about us. Prophetic dreams speak of things not yet seen. Circumstances of our own life can be compared to Scripture. Yet God, who wrote all Scripture, is the same God who gives dreams that He might speak to us. The Bible is absolutely packed with visions and dreams. Scripture helps us to interpret the hidden speech of God, that we might be restored to Him.

*If there is a messenger for him, a mediator, one
among a thousand, to show man His uprightness,*

*Then He is gracious to him, and says, 'deliver
him from going down to the Pit; I have found a
ransom.'*

Job 33:23-24

This speaks of one who has wisdom to interpret, to help bring restoration. We may at times feel like we are all right in God's sight, yet like Job, find that our perception of ourselves is better seen through another light. Study Job 33:1-33, and make notes of what you see and hear. Ask God to please speak to you. Give Him permission to search your soul and see what He will speak. Record your thoughts, or His Words. Later, if you receive a dream, put it in words and record it here for examination.

After asking God to teach you wisdom, allow Him to speak, not just today, but on a daily basis. This will nurture your relationship to spend time waiting and asking for Him to show you through speech (hearing) or dreams (sight). This journey is exciting and should be awesome to look at one year from now!

Our *old man* dreams (and I have had a lot). Yet Paul said that God has chosen the foolish things of this world to put to shame the wise according to the flesh; not many mighty, not many noble are called.

In 1 Corinthians 1:27-29, God's wisdom is revealed.

But God has chosen the foolish things of the world
to put to shame the wise, and God has chosen

the weak things of the world to put to shame the things which are mighty;

and the base things of the world and the things which are despised God has chosen, and the things which are not, to bring to nothing the things that are,

that no flesh should glory in His presence.

1 Corinthians 1:27-29

However, we speak wisdom among those who are mature, yet not the wisdom of this age, nor of the rulers of this age, who are coming to nothing.

But we speak the wisdom of God in a mystery, the hidden wisdom which God ordained before the ages for our glory,

which none of the rulers of this age knew; for had they known, they would not have crucified the Lord of glory.

But as it is written: "Eye has not seen, nor ear heard, nor have entered into the heart of man the things which God has prepared for those who love Him."

But God has revealed them to us through His Spirit. For the Spirit searches all things, yes, the deep things of God.

For what man knows the things of a man except the spirit of the man which is in him? Even so, no one knows the things of God except the Spirit of God.

Now we have received, not the spirit of the world, but the Spirit who is from God, that we might know the things that have been freely given to us by God.

Dreams and Visions

These things we also speak, not in words which man's wisdom teaches but which the Holy Spirit teaches, comparing spiritual things with spiritual.

But the natural man does not receive the things of the Spirit of God, for they are foolishness to him; nor can he know them, because they are spiritually discerned.

But he who is spiritual judges all things, yet he himself is rightly judged by no one.

For "who has known the mind of the Lord that he may instruct Him?" But we have the mind of Christ.

1 Corinthians 2:6-16

We must discern spiritually and interpret spiritually. Many people have had dreams of upcoming events or circumstances and said, *I don't want this. Take it away.* In reality, it was God's hidden speech...His voice leading them.

For we know in part and we prophesy in part.

But when that which is perfect has come, then that which is in part will be done away.

When I was a child, I spoke as a child, I understood as a child, I thought as a child; but when I became a man, I put away childish things.

For now we see in a mirror dimly, but then face to face. Now I know in part, but then I shall know just as I also am known.

And now abide faith, hope, love, these three; but the greatest of these is love.

1 Corinthians 13:9-12

These vows spoken in Verse 11 remain hidden from us as adults, and are sometimes empowered as bitter-root judgments that actually block us from seeing and hearing. It is time to put away childish things and look face to face. A mirror only reflects an image of yourself, and that *dimly*, not in the light of God's Word, and shows those things that are behind you. A dream can actually remove the **veil of limitations** that hinders your relationship with God. If you are only looking at yourself and what you've done in life (good or bad), you block your ability to receive God's best, since He resists the proud [James 4:6 or 1 Peter 5:5] but gives grace to the humble. However, if you allow God to remove the veil or the mirror, then you will know Him even as you are known [1 Corinthians 13:11].

> *Pursue love, and desire spiritual gifts, but especially that you may prophesy.*
>
> *1 Corinthians 14:1*

> *"Then I will come down and talk with you there. I will take of the Spirit that is upon you and will put the same upon them; and they shall bear the burden of the people with you, that you may not bear it yourself alone.*
>
> *"Then you shall say to the people, "Consecrate yourselves for tomorrow, and you shall eat meat;*

for you have wept in the hearing of the Lord, saying, "Who will give us meat to eat? For it was
well with us in Egypt." Therefore the Lord will
give you meat, and you shall eat.

'You shall eat, not one day, nor two days, nor five
days, nor ten days, nor twenty days,

'but for a whole month, until it comes out of your
nostrils and becomes loathsome to you, because
you have despised the Lord who is among you,
and have wept before Him saying, "Why did we
ever come up out of Egypt?'

And Moses said, "The people whom I am among
are six hundred thousand men on foot; yet You
have said, 'I will give them meat, that they may
eat for a whole month.'" Shall flocks and herds
be slaughtered for them, to provide enough for
them? Or shall all the fish of the sea be gathered
together for them, to provide enough for them?"

And the Lord said to Moses, "Has the Lord's arm
been shortened? Now you shall see whether what
I say will happen to you or not."

So Moses went out and told the people the words
of the Lord, and he gathered the seventy men of
the elders of the people and placed them around
the tabernacle.

Then the Lord came down in the cloud, and spoke
to him, and took of the Spirit that was upon him,
and placed the same upon the seventy elders;
and it happened, when the Spirit rested upon
them, that they prophesied, although they never
did so again.

But two men had remained in the camp: the name
of one was El'dad, and the name of the other
Me'dad. And the Spirit rested upon them. Now
they were among those listed, but who had not
gone out to the tabernacle; yet they prophesied
in the camp.

*And a young man ran and told Moses, and said,
"El'dad and Me'dad are prophesying in the camp.*

*So Joshua the son of Nun, Moses' assistant, one
of his choice men, answered and said, "Moses
my lord, forbid them!"*

*Then Moses said to him, "Are you zealous for my
sake? Oh, that all the Lord's people were prophets and that the Lord would put His Spirit upon
them!"*

Numbers 11:17-29

IMPARTATIONS HAPPEN!

This is a powerful picture of impartations! In
Acts 2 we saw an outpouring, but in Numbers 11,
we see another. Prophecy, gifting and wisdom are
all contained in His Spirit. We must cry out for a
watering. As your seed thirsts for Him, cry out for a
watering. As the deer pants for the water brooks,
so pants my soul for you, O God. My soul thirsts for
God, for the living God, when shall I come and ap-
pear before God? Notice we must be crying out for
God even when others say, *Where is your God?* We
can still cry out. See Psalm 42.

We must speak to the rock! Recently I was prophesying and I heard the Lord say, *Speak to the rock
and watch the water come out,* and as I prophesied

to an individual, he began to weep. Suddenly I heard, *Now he has a heart of flesh.* One word from God can melt our stoney hearts. Talk to Him in worship and see if tears don't begin to pour forth. Do it right now! Say *Jesus... You are my rock. Please water me as I water You!*

Not only did God speak in dreams, He is again speaking in this generation just as He always has.

> *Jesus Christ is the same yesterday, today and forever.*
>
> *Hebrews 13:8*

> *"I am the Alpha and the Omega, the Beginning and the End," says the Lord, "who is and who was and who is to come, the Almighty."*
>
> *Revelation 1:8*

> *Saying "I am the Alpha and the Omega, the First and the Last," and "What you see, write in a book and send it to the seven churches, which are in Asia; to Ephesus, to Smyrna, to Pergamos, to Thyatira, to Sardis, to Philadelphia, and to Laodicea."*
>
> *Revelation 1:11*

> *And He said to me, "It is done! I am the Alpha and the Omega, the Beginning and the End. I will give of the fountain of the water of life freely to him who thirsts."*
>
> *Revelation 21:6*

*"I am the Alpha and the Omega, the Beginning
and the End, the First and the Last."*

Revelation 22:13

Sometimes prophetic dreams are for others, for cities, for regions, for nations and for churches. However, I could counsel you to always start with.... *God, what are you saying to me, about me?* Jesus will give of the fountain of the water of life freely to him who thirsts as in Revelation 21:6.

*"He who overcomes shall inherit all things, and I
will be his God and he shall be my Son."*

Revelation 21:7

*"And behold, I am coming quickly, and My reward
is with Me, to give to every one according to his
work.*

*"I am the Alpha and the Omega, the Beginning
and the End, the First and the Last."*

*Blessed are those who do His commandments,
that they may have the right to the tree of life,
and may enter through the gates into the city.*

Revelation 22:12-14

I once dreamed a dream that was amazingly simple and yet amusing. I dreamed I was walking along a path, and suddenly I saw two very bright and somewhat glowing individuals looking at each other. They were facing one another with flaming swords drawn and held over head, tip to tip forming a sort of triangle. I noticed my path was about to go right under their swords. Fear began to grip my spirit, yet I felt I should proceed. Suddenly I walked right in between them under their swords and they both smiled. Until they smiled, I actually felt a little intimidated. Suddenly as I passed through, it was if my eyes saw for the first time, two trees, one on the left and one on the right. I heard *choose* (notice I both saw and heard). I chose the tree on the left and suddenly a hand appeared pouring oil on the tree. Amusingly I heard *Rise up; make yourself a salad.* I began to reach out for the leaves dripping with oil. I placed them to my mouth and found upon awakening that my hand was to my mouth. I actually felt strengthened and began receiving incredible insight as the Word came alive. Notice in Genesis 3:24, the cherubims were guarding the tree of life.

> So He drove out the man; and He placed cherubim at the east of the garden of Eden, and a flaming sword which turned every way, to guard the way to the tree of life.
>
> *Genesis 3:24*
>
> "And behold, I am coming quickly, and My reward is with Me, to give to every one according to his work. I am the Alpha and the Omega, the Beginning and the End, the First and the Last.

Blessed are those who do His commandments,
that they may have the right to the tree of life,
and may enter through the gates into the city."

Revelation 22:12-14

Notice there is a blessing to those who keep His commandments, that they may have the right to the tree of life and may enter through the gates into the city!

Dreams and Visions

Chapter Four

Interpretation of Symbols

The hidden speech of God is amazingly simple and most complex. God will use rhymes, themes, and colors, just about anything imaginable, and speech that is so complex that it will cause you to see things years later that will continue to grow in you if you will allow it. As with any gift, if you do not use it, it may be taken away and given to another. Mark 4 is a powerful key to the development of faith in the heart; a key to receive, if you will.

We are endeavoring to impart a very practical means of discovering the will of God. As a prophetic ministry, our approach may be somewhat different in scope or nature than others. However, God is Spirit and those who worship the Father must worship Him in Spirit and Truth. Therefore, what we may label as prophetic may indeed be a spiritual approach, but also a scriptural approach. We desire to compare spiritual to spiritual; line upon line, precept upon precept. This is why we have desired to lay or *throw down* a solid foundation. Remembering always to pray for discernment and interpretations to be godly in nature.

The Lord can be very amusing, and in our ministry, symbols, types, shadows, and visions are very helpful, and because God is the voice of many waters, we see clearly that He *echoes* His speech. In other words, the same symbols once taught as prophetic language, and learned, may at times be used over and over. However, when interpreting another's dreams, I personally found that a *fire truck* in one man's speech may be a symbol of *alarm or warning*, and to another man, a sign of *rage or anger* screaming with sirens and bells as it speeds down the road. However, to another it could be symbolic of help sent to extinguish a situation that would otherwise destroy.

So as you see, proper perspective is extremely important. It may require you to *know* the one you are speaking to in order to give a correct interpretation. There were actually a few people who were gifted to interpret dreams....Joseph and Daniel are two that immediately come to mind. For Joseph declared, *Do not interpretations belong to God? Tell them to me, please.*

It came to pass after these things that the butler and the baker of the king of Egypt offended their lord, the king of Egypt.

And Pharaoh was angry with his two officers, the chief butler and the chief baker.

So he put them in custody in the house of the captain of the guard, in the prison, the place where Joseph was confined.

And the captain of the guard charged Joseph with them, and he served them; so they were in custody for a while.

Then the butler and the baker of the king of Egypt, who were confined in the prison, had a dream, both of them, each man's dream in one night and each man's dream with its own interpretation.

And Joseph came in to them in the morning and looked at them, and saw that they were sad.

So he asked Pharaoh's officers who were with him in the custody of his lord's house, saying, "Why do you look so sad today?"

And they said to him, "We each have had a dream, and there is no interpreter of it." So Joseph said to them, "Do not interpretations belong to God? Tell them to me, please."

Then the chief baker told his dream to Joseph, and said to him, "Behold, in my dream a vine was before me,

"and in the vine were three branches; it was as though it budded, its blossoms shot forth, and its clusters brought forth ripe grapes.

"Then Pharaoh's cup was in my hand; and I took the grapes and pressed them into Pharaoh's cup, and placed the cup in Pharaoh's hand."

Dreams and Visions

And Joseph said to him, "This is the interpretation of it: The three branches are three days.

"Now within three days Pharaoh will lift up your head and restore you to your place, and you will put Pharaoh's cup in his hand according to the former manner, when you were his butler.

"But remember me when it is well with you, and please show kindness to me; make mention of me to Pharaoh, and get me out of this house.

"For indeed I was stolen away from the land of the Hebrews; and also I have done nothing here that they should put me into the dungeon."

When the chief butler saw that the interpretation was good, he said to Joseph, "I also was in my dream, and there were three white baskets on my head.

"In the uppermost basket were all kinds of baked goods for Pharaoh, and the birds ate them out of the basket on my head."

So Joseph answered and said, "This is the interpretation of it: The three baskets are three days.

"Within three days Pharaoh will lift off your head from you and hang you on a tree; and the birds will eat your flesh from you."

Now it came to pass on the third day, which was Pharaoh's birthday, that he made a feast for all his servants; and he lifted up the head of the chief butler and of the chief baker among his servants.

Then he restored the chief butler to his butlership again, and he placed the cup in Pharaoh's hand.

But he hanged the chief baker, as Joseph had interpreted to them.

Yet the chief butler did not remember Joseph, but forgot him."

Genesis 40:1-23

In Genesis 40:1-7 we see two men who caused an offense to the king of Egypt who placed them in prison. These were worldly men who needed *a gift* from God. This is a perfect example of *For God so loved the world that He sent His only begotten Son...* It is a wonderful prophetic promise that God sent a gift to save and restore. Dreams are seeds of restoration when watered with the Word of God, and seen through His eyes they bring great peace.

When Joseph declared *Do not interpretations belong to God? Tell them to me, please,* he was declaring *that His* Spirit has sent me here to help you! In other words, I know the nature of God as He speaks symbolically. Symbols are hidden speech, which can be used thousands of years later. As you can see, it would be really important for the *right* interpretation to come forth. Joseph's dream in Genesis 37:1-11 shows us **Prophetic destiny.**

> *Now Jacob dwelt in the land where his father was a stranger, in the land of Canaan.*
>
> *This is the history of Jacob. Joseph, being seventeen years old, was feeding the flock with his brothers. And the lad was with the sons of Bil'hah and the sons of Zilpah, his father's wives; and Joseph brought a bad report of them to his father.*
>
> *Now Israel loved Joseph more than all his children, because he was the son of his old age. Also, he made him a tunic of many colors.*

69

Dreams and Visions

But when his brothers saw that their father loved him more than all his brothers, they hated him and could not speak peaceably to him.

Now Joseph had a dream, and he told it to his brothers; and they hated him even more.

So he said to them, "Please hear this dream which I have dreamed:

"There we were, binding sheaves in the field. Then behold my sheaf arose and also stood upright; and indeed your sheaves stood all around and bowed down to my sheaf."

And his brothers said to him, "Shall you indeed reign over us? Or shall you indeed have dominion over us?" So they hated him even more for his dreams and for his words.

Then he dreamed still another dream and told it to his brothers, and said, "Look, I have dreamed another dream. And this time, the sun, the moon, and the eleven stars bowed down to me."

So he told it to his father and his brothers; and his father rebuked him and said to him, "What is this dream that you have dreamed? Shall your mother and I and your brothers indeed come to bow down to the earth before you?"

And his brothers envied him, but his father kept the matter in mind."

Genesis 37:1-11

Genesis 37:1-11

OBSERVATIONS:

The power of life and death are in our tongues. We will literally eat the fruit of our lips.

Genesis 42:25-38
Simeon is Held in Egypt

OBSERVATIONS:

Genesis 43:1-34
Jacob's Sons Return To Egypt

OBSERVATIONS:

Dreams and Visions

Genesis 37:12-36

OBSERVATIONS:

Genesis 41:1-46
Joseph Interprets Dreams/Pharaoh's Dreams

OBSERVATIONS:

Genesis 41:37-57
Joseph's Rise to Power

OBSERVATIONS:

Genesis 42:1-24
Jacob's Sons Go To Egypt

OBSERVATIONS:

Genesis 44:1-17
Judah Pleads for Benjamin

OBSERVATIONS:

Genesis 44:18-34
Joseph Identifies Himself

OBSERVATIONS:

Genesis 45:1-28
A Reunion of Brothers

OBSERVATIONS:

Genesis 46:1-27
Jacob Moves To Egypt

OBSERVATIONS:

Genesis 46:28-34
Jacob Settles in Goshen

OBSERVATIONS:

Genesis 47:1-12
Famine in the land of Egypt

OBSERVATIONS:

Genesis 47:13-26 Joseph Rules During Famine

OBSERVATIONS:

Genesis 47:27-31
Joseph's Vow to Jacob

OBSERVATIONS:

Genesis 48:1-22
The Blessing of Restoration

OBSERVATIONS:

INTERPRETATIONS BELONG TO GOD!

This *Dreams and Visions* book is not a replacement for a relationship with the Creator, it is only a tool for helping us to begin to tap into the unlimited supply of His Grace and Wisdom! While there are many useful tools available, this message deals more with watering our dream seeds and allowing the hidden potential of God's dream for our lives to shine forth and cause us to focus on our destiny. Prophecy is the foretelling or unveiling of that seed (in part). We must actively and aggressively water the seeds to refresh us. In doing so, we will eventually discover the hidden potential of God's treasure inside each of us.

It is God's desire to restore right thinking in a heart that is yielded to Him. We cannot *live* by our thoughts or ideas. *True* life comes from a relationship that is rooted in God's principles. <u>*God's mind is a terrible thing to waste!*</u> Our mind contains knowledge that is obtained or gathered from life experiences. We rely on *reason* as the basis by which we establish a theory. However, theory and reasoning are NOT the source of the Holy Spirit. Reasoning short circuits God by developing a trust in SELF that is independent of our sense perceptions. We must begin to *enthrone* the Spirit of the Lord in our minds, and begin to realize that *His knowledge* can be transmitted *Spirit to Spirit.*

But as it is written: "Eye has not seen, nor ear heard, nor have entered into the heart of man the things which God has prepared for those who love Him."

1 Corinthians 2:9

Christ is the power and wisdom of God!

For the message of the cross is foolishness to those who are perishing, but to us who are being saved it is the power of God.

For it is written: "I will destroy the wisdom of the wise, and bring to nothing the understanding of the prudent."

Where is the wise? Where is the scribe? Where is the disputer of this age? Has not God made foolish the wisdom of this world?

For since, in the wisdom of God, the world through wisdom did not know God, it pleased God through the foolishness of the message preached to save those who believe.

For Jews request a sign, and Greeks seek after wisdom;

but we preach Christ crucified, to the Jews a stumbling block and to the Greeks foolishness, but to those who are called, both Jews and Greeks, Christ the power of God and the wisdom of God.

Because the foolishness of God is wiser than men, and the weakness of God is stronger than men.

For you see your calling, brethren, that not many wise according to the flesh, not many mighty, not many noble, are called.

But God has chosen the foolish things of the world to put to shame the wise, and God has chosen the weak things of the world to put to shame the things which are mighty;

and the base things of the world and the things which are despised God has chosen, and the things which are not, to bring to nothing the things that are, that no flesh should glory in His presence.

But of Him you are in Christ Jesus, who became for us wisdom from God—and righteousness and sanctification and redemption—

that, as it is written, "He who glories, let him glory in the Lord,"

                              1 Corinthians 1:18-31

"And I, brethren, when I came to you, did not come with excellence of speech or of wisdom declaring to you the testimony of God.

For I determined not to know anything among you except Jesus Christ and Him crucified.

I was with you in weakness, in fear, and in much trembling.

And my speech and my preaching were not with persuasive words of human wisdom, but in demonstration of the Spirit and of power, that your faith should not be in the wisdom of men but in the power of God.

However, we speak wisdom among those who are mature, yet not the wisdom of this age, nor of the rulers of this age, who are coming to nothing.

But we speak the wisdom of God in a mystery, the hidden wisdom which God ordained before the ages for our glory,

which none of the rulers of this age knew; for had they known, they would not have crucified the Lord of glory.

But as it is written: "Eye has not seen, nor ear heard, nor have entered into the heart of man the things which God has prepared for those who love Him."

But God has revealed them to us through His Spirit. For the Spirit searches all things, yes, the deep things of God.

For what man knows the things of a man except the spirit of the man which is in Him? Even so no one knows the things of God except the Spirit of God.

Now we have received, not the spirit of the world, but the Spirit who is from God, that we might know the things that have been freely given to us by God.

These things we also speak, not in words which man's wisdom teaches, but which the Holy Spirit teaches, comparing spiritual things with spiritual.

But the natural man does not receive the things of the Spirit of God, for they are foolishness to him; nor can he know them, because they are spiritually discerned.

But he who is spiritual judges all things, yet he himself is rightly judged by no one.

For "who has known the mind of the Lord that he may instruct Him?" But we have the mind of Christ."

1 Corinthians 2:1-16

God is calling for us to use both the mind and the Spirit. Many times we find in Christianity, people who are using one or the other. We have all met (and even operated at times ourselves) people who use analytical thought processes to TRY to discern the *Spirit*, as well as those who are spiritual but don't use common sense. Jesus desires to restore us as humans to the Father of all Creation. In this restoration, we become balanced once again. People who use only the Word can become selective in their reasoning and embrace a partial truth yet be void of spiritual life.

In John 5:37-40,42, we see a prophetic picture of Jesus saying to us that if we do not have His Word ABIDING in us, we don't really believe at all.

And the Father Himself, who sent Me, has testified of Me. You have neither heard His voice at any time, nor seen His form.

But you do not have His word abiding in you, because whom I Ie sent, I Iim you do not believe.

> But you are not willing to come to Me that you
> may have life."
>
> "But I know you, that you do not have the love of
> God in you."
>
> John 5:37-40,42

That's powerful! In essence, He says, *You know the Word in your mind, but not in your heart. So I am not living in you. I am only walking with you, waiting...for you to let My life come into you.*

I heard the Lord say recently that there were many pall-bearers in the church. As I inquired, the Lord showed me groups of people asking permission to remove Jesus from the Cross and carry Him to a tomb (their heart). However, they have not truly progressed to realize the revelation of Him removing the handkerchief from their eyes to see the light. He removed their grave clothes and now He is a living Jesus, alive in their hearts. Where is the true evidence of His life abiding in us as we abide in Him? God is calling us to go beyond the world's view of Christianity which rationalizes His death and burial, and come to a living stone. This will bring us into a true spiritual encounter with the light of God's truth illuminating our hearts and causing us to fall in love with a living Jesus. A fusion of spirits with power and strength comes from communion in dreams and visions as we see and hear and become eyewitnesses of His resurrection power going about doing good as we see His power to heal, to deliver, to cleanse, and to raise the dead. I will raise the dead because He lives in me. It's time to SEE yourself speaking to a dead stinking body and declaring **COME FORTH!** Jesus said, *Come to Me that you may have life.* We <u>must</u> be willing.

True communion with God is His deepest desire. Communion is common-union. Hebrews 12:18-26 says we cannot turn away God who is speaking from heaven, yet His Kingdom is in our heart. Listen to Him right now!

> *For you have not come to the mountain that may be touched and that burned with fire, and to blackness and darkness and tempest,*
>
> *and the sound of a trumpet and the voice of words, so that those who heard it begged that the word should not be spoken to them anymore.*
>
> *(For they could not endure what was commanded: "And if so much as a beast touches the mountain, it shall be stoned or shot with an arrow."*
>
> *And so terrifying was the sight that Moses said, "I am exceedingly afraid and trembling.")*
>
> *But you have come to Mount Zion and to the city of the living God, the heavenly Jerusalem, to an innumerable company of angels,*

to the general assembly and church of the first-born who are registered in heaven, to God the Judge of all, to the spirits of just men made perfect,

to Jesus the Mediator of a new covenant, and to the blood sprinkling that speaks of better things than that of Abel.

See that you do not refuse Him who speaks. For if they did not escape who refused Him who spoke on earth, much more shall we not escape if we turn away from Him who speaks from heaven,

whose voice then shook the earth; but now He has promised, saying, "Yet once more I shake not only the earth, but also heaven."

Hebrews 12:18-26

Then He said, "Hear now My words: If there is a prophet among you, I, the Lord, make Myself known to him in a vision; I speak to him in a dream."

Numbers 12:6

This is a spiritual picture of a visionary.

Then Jesus answered and said to them, "Most assuredly, I say to you, the Son can do nothing of Himself, but what He sees the Father do, for whatever He does, the Son also does in like manner."

John 5:19

Look at all of the various references to dreams and visions, as well as, seers who see, who look or refer to our eyes.

> *"The lamp of the body is the eye. If therefore, your eye is good, your whole body will be full of light (revelation)."*
>
> *Matthew 6:22*

Study 1 Corinthians 12:1-27, and see how God uses ALL of the gifts through ALL of the Body.

> *If the whole body were an eye, where would be the hearing? If the whole were hearing, where would be the smelling?*
>
> *1 Corinthians 12:17*

Dreams and Visions

Some of the Ways/Principles of God's Speech
Scriptural Study References

Genesis 3:5-8 — Look, saw, and heard (Eve)

Genesis 15:1-6 — A vision came as Abraham looked

Genesis 18:1-3 — Abraham saw as the Lord appeared.

Genesis 20:6: — Abimelech dreamed (he heard)

Genesis 20:11 — Abraham heard the angel from heaven.

Genesis 22:15 — Abraham heard the angel from heaven
a second time.

Genesis 26:2 — The Lord appeared to Isaac

Genesis 28:13-15 — Jacob hears God

Genesis 30:41 — A prophet puts a rod before the eyes so they
conceive

Genesis 31:10-13 — Angel of God speaks in a dream to
Jacob

Genesis 31:24 — God visits Laban in a dream (warning)

Genesis 35:1 — God speaks to Jacob

Genesis 37:5 — Joseph dreams big

Genesis 37:8 — Hated for your dreams (rejection therapy)

Genesis 37:19 — Ungodly people recognize true dreamers

Genesis 40:5 — Butler/Baker dreams

Genesis 40:6 — Joseph sees ministry opportunity

Genesis 41:1-5 — Two dreams

Genesis 41:9-13 — Faith for true interpretations come

Genesis 41:17 — Pharaoh tells dreams to Joseph

Genesis 41:26 — True interpretations come

Genesis 46:2 — God speaks to Israel in night visions

Genesis 49:22 — Prophecy of a fruitful bough (Joseph)

Exodus 3:2-22 — Angel of the Lord appears to Moses with
instructions

Exodus 4:1-24 — Moses fellowships with great intensity with God

Exodus 4:27 — God speaks to Aaron with instructions

Exodus 16:10 — Glory appears

Exodus 24:15 — Moses enters the Glory

Exodus 24:17 — Children of Israel see the sight

Exodus 24:18 — Moses enters the midst of the Cloud

Numbers 21:8 — Instructions to live: Look!

Numbers 22:23 — Even donkeys see visions!

Numbers 22:28 — Even donkeys can speak for God!

Numbers 22:31 — God can use donkeys to open eyes!

Numbers 24:1-4 — Eyes open, visions of God. Hear it!

Numbers 24:16 — Eyes open, ears open, see visions!

Deuteronomy 13:1-5 — Discernment for true prophetic dreams!

Deuteronomy 29:3 — Our eyes were meant to see

Deuteronomy 29:4 — God must help us to perceive and hear!

Joshua 5:13-15 — Joshua sees, looks, beholds and listens!

Judges 6:11-23 — Joshua receives instructions from the angel of the Lord

Judges 7:13 — Enemies even dream of your greatness

Judges 13:16-21 — Angel appears to Manoah (he sees)

Judges 14:12-14 — Samson poses a riddle

Judges 14:16 — Prophets/judges can interpret riddles!

Judges 16:7 — God speaks in enigmas (mysteries/tight knots)

1 Samuel 2:3 — God weighs our speech

1 Samuel 3:1 — As we minister to the Lord, revelation comes

1 Samuel 3:2 — Eli's eyes dim

1 Samuel 3:4 — Samuel hears God's voice

1 Samuel 3:11 — Prophetic revelation comes to Samuel

1 Samuel 9:11 — Seers sought!

1 Samuel 9:16 — God anoints seers!

1 Samuel 9:19 — Interpreters see because they're anointed

Dreams and Visions

1 Samuel 28:6 — There are times God is silent, keep asking God!

1 Samuel 28:15 — We must only inquire of God

2 Samuel 7:4-10 — Word of the Lord comes to Nathan

2 Samuel 7:14 — Prophecy comes by visions to kings

2 Samuel 15:27 — Seers

2 Samuel 24:11-12— Gad, David's seer with choices from God

1 Kings 3:5-15 — Solomon has a dream to ask for wisdom

1 Kings 6:11-17 — Solomon builds what he hears—Word of the Lord comes

2 Kings 17:2 — Word of the Lord comes to Elijah

2 Kings 17:13 — Authority to declare

1 Chron. 9:22— Seers were governmentally appointed

1 Chron. 17:3-15 — Prophets are directed in night seasons

1 Chron. 17:16 — Kings respond to prophetic words

Job 4:12 — God's Spirit visits in the night with whispers

Job 7:14 — Job complains of scary dreams/visions

Job 9:14 — Job wonders about reasoning with God

Job 13:1-3 — Job speaks about reasoning with God

Job 33:14-18 — God speaks in dreams and seals instructions

Psalm 5:1-3 — David directs his heart to God

Psalm 13:3 — David pleas with God to enlighten his eyes

Psalm 23:5 — Communion with God

Psalm 25:1-6 — Plea to know God

Psalm 27:11 — Plea to be taught

Psalm 28:1-2 — Plea to be heard

Psalm 31:2 — Plea for deliverance

Psalm 33:3-4 — Communion with God—He is Good

Psalm 33:6 — Heavens made by breath of God

Psalm 36:7-9 — Water and Light from God

Psalm 40:3 — God waters David with Life

Psalm 42:7— Deep calls to deep

Psalm 44:23 — Cry to God to Wake Up! Hunger!

Psalm 66:16-19 — God hears our voice!

Psalm 89:19-20 — David anointed to see visions

Psalm 101:2-3 — Covenant with your eyes

Psalm 105:15 — God protects prophets

Psalm 119:18 — God opens eyes to see

Psalm 119:133 — God directs our steps with His Word

Psalm 123:1-2 — Place your eyes on God: face to face

Psalm 141:8-9 — Keep eyes on God

Psalm 143:8-10 — God causes us to hear each morning

Proverbs 4:1-27 — Get wisdom! Hear it!

Proverbs 5:21 — God sees you

Proverbs 7:24 — Hear God's words of His mouth

Proverbs 15:14 — Our hearts seek understanding/knowledge

Proverbs 16:9 — God directs our steps

Proverbs 16:25 — Our ways bring death

Proverbs 21:1 — The Lord guides our heart

Proverbs 23:26 — Give God your heart

Proverbs 25:13 — Your words refresh others

Proverbs 29:3 — Please God, Love Wisdom

Ecclesiastes 4:13-16 — Joseph, Rags to Riches

Ecclesiastes 5:3 — Activity; dreams

Ecclesiastes 5:7 — Many dreams/fear God

Song of Solomon 3:1 — Keep seeking

Isaiah 1:1 — Visions Happen!

Isaiah 6:1-8 — Visions of Glory

Isaiah 8:18 — Signs & Wonders

Isaiah 17:7 — Our eyes respect our Maker

Dreams and Visions

100

Dreams and Visions

PRODUCT LISTING
Audio Tapes Series:

__ Dreams & Visions/Language of the Spirit 4-in	$20
__ Birthing & Becoming Sons & Daughters 8-in	$40
__ Preparing For The Call 8-in	$40
__ Watchman, What of the Night? 8-in	$40
__ The Gift of Prophecy 6-in	$30
__ The Book of Acts Unfolded 6-in	$30
__ Answering the Call 6-in	$30
__ Exposing Jezebel's Table 4-in	$20
__ The Just Shall Live By Faith 4-in	$20
__ Prophecy Unlocks Destiny 4-in	$20
__ Understanding Your Dreams/Visions 4-in	$20
__ Establishing a Firm Foundation 2-in	$15
__ Building the House of God 2-in	$15
__ Discerning the Battle 2-in	$15
__ Stirring Up the Gift 2-in	$15
__ 30, 60, 100-Fold 2-in	$15
__ Freedom From Famine 2-in	$15
__ Positioning the Watchman 2-in	$15
__ God Tears Down To Build Up 2-in	$15
__ Releasing The Prophetic 2-in	$15
__ Breaking Ungodly Soul Ties 2-in	$15
__ New Foundations for New Believers 2-in	$15

Books:

__ Dreams & Visions/Language of the Spirit	$19.95
__ Supernatural Dreams and Visions	$24.95
__ Prophesying the Heart of God (booklet)	$ 4.00

LCMI's first prophetic worship cd....
LIVE!

from Bermuda...Will you say, you will...

____ CD $15   ____ Cassette $10

Videos:

__ *Dreams & Visions/Language of the Spirit*
two tape set $40

LCMI's first prophetic worship cd....
LIVE!

from Bermuda...Will you say, you will...

____ CD $15   ____ Cassette $10

Videos:

__ *Dreams & Visions/Language of the Spirit*
two tape set $40

Look for "Live" Web Broadcasts direct from

Prophetic Connections International Church

At WWW.STUDIO153.COM.

DVD's & CD's available soon. Write for a free catalog.

Additional materials are available on audio, video, cd or dvd.

To Purchase by Phone using Credit
Card,
Call (734) 782-5128
Please include $3.50 for postage and
handling.

To Purchase by Fax using Credit Card,
Make a copy of the Product Listing
page and
Fax it to (734) 782-5194
Please include $3.50 for postage and
handling.

To Purchase by Mail,
Make a copy of the Product Listing
page and

Send it along with check or money
order to:
Life Changes Ministries Int'l
P.O. Box 153
New Boston, MI 48164
Please include $3.50 for postage and
handling.

To Purchase by Website using Credit
Card,
Visit WWW.BOBGRIFFINWORLD.COM
Please include $3.50 for postage and
handling.